D1370710

Hangin' Out

This book is for four parents who were once children.
And didn't forget.
Helen and Fred
Betty and Hugh

Hangin' Out

City Kids, City Games

Written and Photographed by

James Wagenvoord

Designed by Anita Wagenvoord

J. B. Lippincott Company
Philadelphia and New York

Copyright © 1974 by James Wagenvoord
All rights reserved
First edition
Printed in the United States of America

The quotation from *Let Us Now Praise Famous Men* by James
Agee and Walker Evans is reprinted with the permission
of Houghton Mifflin Company.

The quotation from *The City in History* by Lewis Mumford
is reprinted by permission of Harcourt Brace Jovanovich, Inc.

U.S. Library of Congress Cataloging in Publication Data

Wagenvoord, James.
 Hangin' out: city kids, city games.

 SUMMARY: Text and photographs present the
street games of city children.
 1. Games. [1. Games] I. Title.
GV1203.W26 1974   793.4   73-16293
ISBN-0-397-01028-1

acknowledgments

A few years ago Dmitri Kessel, one of the gentlest people I will ever know and one of the finest photographers who has ever focused a camera, gave me my first good piece of equipment and the challenge to work with it. If the photography in this book begins to do justice to an aspect of growing up in a city, it is in large measure due to him.

I think that anyone who makes a thing called a book should thank William Saroyan. He, perhaps more than any other man, understands and honors the form and, whether he wants to or not, represents honesty. Thank you, Mr. Saroyan.

It would take a companion volume twice the length of this book to name the city people of all ages who helped make this book happen. Thomas, Tom, Carl, Ronald, Harold, Julio, Bonita, Joey, Moppy, Choo Choo, Paulette, Ernestine, Otis, Rat, Janet, Buddha, Rosita, Robert, Poopie, Raoul, Pete, Jesus, Peanuts, Mike, Bill, Angel, Stevie, and all of you who took my wanderings around the blocks for granted and taught me things about cities, thanks. And Anita, Fumio, Bob, Victor, Mitch, and Eleanor—I'm in your debt.

James Wagenvoord

PROPERTY OF
TAKOMA PARK, MD. LIBRARY
83307

“ In every child who is born, under no matter what circumstances, and of no matter what parents, the potentiality of the human race is born again: and in him, too, once more, and in each of us, our terrific responsibility towards human life; towards the utmost idea of ” goodness, of the horror of error, and of God.

—James Agee, *Let Us Now Praise Famous Men*

contents

city kids, city games

This book began for me early last summer while riding east on a North Carolina State highway from Charlotte to Spivey's Corner. I had thought about it and discussed it a few weeks earlier, but when I began the drive to North Carolina to work up a magazine piece about a small county fair I had decided not to work on it. I'd had enough of the city.

Riding on a lightly traveled road in early evening, heading through the Carolina tobacco region, I was still mulling over the reasons why I didn't want to do a book about city kids and games. The air in that part of the state in the hour or so that links late afternoon with dusk takes on a crystalline quality. The sun had begun its long, slow dive toward night, and as the early summer heat slipped away, the land and the houses and barns, accented by long shadows stretching east, shouted with color. I was looking toward a small house at the crest of a long rise, separated from the road by a melon patch. In front of the house a girl, three, maybe four years old at the most, wearing an oatmeal-colored cardigan sweater, bent down in the patch. And as we drove past the house she shoved two small melons up under her sweater, stood up, and broke into a smile, a huge open smile that comes all too often only with the laughter of children. She turned and, holding her new-found adult shape, ran as quickly as she could—the smile growing even brighter—toward the house. I decided I would try to do a book about city kids.

After returning to the city, I began paying
attention to urban games and pastimes and to
the city as a place where children grow up
and discover and nurture fantasy—and, if
they're lucky, survive. The thread was the
games of the street believed by city people to be
unique to their cities: stickball, stoopball,
ringolevio, the kind of things that fit into
middle-class conversation as buzz words indi-
cating a knowledge of growing up in a city. The
street games, though, are secondary to the
players. The games themselves are only a framework and one element of growing up in the
heart of an American city. The lack of organized
structure, the limits on space, and the passing
from generation to generation of the forms
themselves, with room for the specifics to be
added on by the current generation of players,
are what give the games their unique qualities.

I had seen games being played on the streets
for years—ever since I had moved to the city
from a quiet Iowa town. I had lingered occasionally for a minute or two on the sidelines of
a stickball game, and I had missed a step on a
sidewalk waiting for a stoopball game to clear
long enough to be allowed to pass through the
players and get on toward a destination. I had
traded brief looks with random rope jumpers
and been intimidated by small groups of teen-
agers. Always, though, I was in strange territory.
To look now, to really pay attention, and to become familiar with the players was to experience
an unexpected mix of emotion.

The city that I, growing up in the Midwest, had dreamed of living in didn't include crowded neighborhoods. In Cedar Rapids, Iowa, in the fifties, the dream of an attainable city was focused on Omaha. Chicago was the fantasy in the more brazen daydreams, and when really letting go—New York! It was the time of Doris Day movies and Dan Dailey movies. Slouched in a cracked oilcloth-covered seat in the State Theater, I would marvel at opening scenes showing Gig Young or William Holden stepping out of a limousine on a bustling midtown Manhattan street and striding toward a shiny office skyscraper. He would move through an archway, past a brass plaque with the words, THE WINDSOR BUILDING, and a doorman would nod to the star and say, "Good morning, Mr. Windsor."

City kids? The Bowery Boys filled part of that fantasy, and the rest was made up of visions of the perennial European grandfather, S. Z. Sakall, giving Doris Day advice on how to be honest to the rich young man who sought her hand and would still love her—perhaps love her even more—when he learned of her humble beginnings. The kids in Doris's neighborhood wore caps and knickers and ran across the screen shouting happily. Everything wasn't completely up, of course. Occasionally someone in grainy black and white, like the young John Derek, would give a glimpse of the sadness and hardship that could come with actually growing up in a city. The early realism and even the movie version of *The Amboy Dukes* with gang wars

and perspiring sex longings would fade against
the color and bounce of big-budget musicals and
light comedies that helped to make me certain
by my fourteenth birthday that a city—a real
city—was the only place to live.

Lewis Mumford in *The City in History* states,
"The chief function of the city is to convert
power into form, energy into culture, dead matter into the living symbols of art, biological re-
production into social creativity. The positive
functions of the city cannot be performed without
creating new institutional arrangements, capable
of coping with the vast energies modern man
now commands: arrangements just as bold as
those that originally transform the overgrown
village and its stronghold into the city."

In the United States of the seventies, the
city instead of fulfilling such functions has become, from a subjective viewpoint, a nightmare—
viewed, that is, from the suburbs or a medium-
size town. For the imagery being fed into towns
such as Cedar Rapids, Iowa, through daily
flashes on television screens rather than weekly
movies, is not that excitement and fortune waits
for you in the cities, but danger. You can get
mugged there. You probably will, and people
will just stand by and watch it happen to you.
There's a lot of graft, a lot of corruption, and
drugs on every street corner. The point that gets
not only pushed aside but is erased by most
reports is that one hell of a lot of living is going
on. There are tremendous problems, but there
are families in the cities, and children are being
born and trying to grow up. They're out there on

the stoops and in the streets with dreams, energy, and toughness. Kids are watching and learning and playing and fighting with each other and for survival, getting ready to be legal grown-ups. In watching them and learning from them, it might be possible to remember what it was we grown-ups started out to be and to do when we were aware of new things in a world that promised to grow large instead of smothering us.

I walked through a city. I sat on a stoop on Madison Street in Brooklyn on a gray, gusty fall afternoon. Within one hundred feet of my vantage point there was a three-man touch football game being played out; some boys flinging homemade miniature parachutes a few feet up toward the scudding clouds; rope jumpers; two sisters—the older seven—drawing hearts and peace symbols with colored chalk on the sidewalk; and in the middle of the street a no-holds-barred game of street hockey went on for three professional twenty-minute periods. Down on the corner an abandoned refrigerator was being loudly taken apart by some of the hockey players' younger brothers and sisters. Nothing had been scheduled, and there were no official supervisors. It was terrific.

I watched and photographed the "little kids" jumping rope on East 155th Street in the crowded south Bronx. Over three hundred families live on that single New York block; you can walk it in one hundred and fifty steps. The girls were jumping, counting it off. They soared and skipped and soared. S. Z. Sakall and Doris Day were nowhere to be found. Life was on those

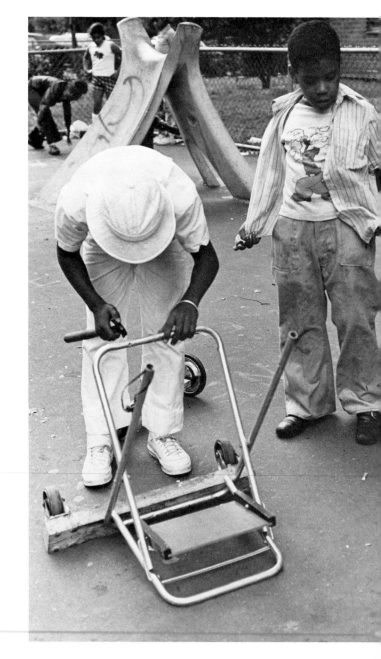

streets, and joy, in the ropes and in a handball game going on against a wall a few feet from the jumpers. I felt disgust at the garbage and litter that a city bureaucracy ignores except once a week. And anger that the kids on streets such as this, threading city generations together through their play, are faced constantly throughout their young lives with the specter of drugs. And I saw the street fear caused by drugs as commerce. Not to get involved with drugs seems to require of a city kid almost superhuman self-discipline and an equal amount of luck. This is not news. The growth of drugs has become a story so consistent and firm in the media that everyone knows it—the way everyone knew the Indochina war was there year after year after year after year. Like the war, its exposure may have exhausted media's target, the white middle-class non-user. On the streets, the awareness is of a different level. Considerably more electric, it can't be put away with the click of a television knob.

I stayed on the streets and in the neighborhood playgrounds, and I stayed away from organized programs and the large city parks. It was not because I felt that the programs and the people who coordinate them weren't important. On the contrary, the work of the community-center summer day camps and their year-long programs, the Police Athletic League—particularly their no-traffic play streets—the Parks Department summer neighborhood recreation programs, the beginnings of open tennis instructional clinics, to name only a few efforts, stand

out as relatively selfless things that are available for people growing up in a city. I stayed on the streets because they are always in play for whoever wants them. They don't open at nine and close at three-thirty, they are available every day regardless of seasons and national holidays, and they're where life starts and ends for many city people.

I didn't photograph or see many of the games and pastimes that are talked about often by people who grew up in cities fifteen or twenty years ago: punchball, for instance, or wink, tag-one-tag-all, and capture the flag. I'm certain that right now someone is playing them as well as countless other games. I just didn't run into them. I simply began walking in the summer and kept walking until the change from day-light saving time to standard time took away real afternoons. I photographed situations as they occurred, rather than in alphabetical order or against a preconceived table of contents. Much of it is in this book. And ideally the way to look at this book would be to tear it apart, shuffle the pictures, and just leaf through them. That's how city kids play their games, moving quickly from one to another, back again, then on to yet another. Some are played in beat to professional sports seasons, but most overlap and demolish any attempt to create a form with a calendar.

I thought I'd had enough of the city before
I began walking. I was wrong. A lot of smug
assumptions fell apart. I saw and heard a great
deal of tough, tempered street wisdom. I became
angrier than I thought possible about how many
of the people who live in cities are exploited
and discarded by so many of the people who are
in positions to run cities and who profit from
them. I witnessed parents give of themselves to
an unimagined degree. I began to learn and
know from street and youth workers who care
and who do help people to survive and sometimes
to win out, and I was permitted to view for brief
moments the dreams and fantasies of many
people. And I realized something. I'm not a
tourist. I live here. It beats the hell out of the
fifties movies.

PROPERTY OF
TAKOMA PARK, MD. LIBRARY
83307

Walking.

Down 95th Street.

Lou Gehrig was born just a couple of blocks away. Over on 94th. There's a plaque, weathered and stained, on the front of a laundry building that says so. Came off the streets of the city and earned his place as a baseball immortal.

The big guys on 95th are playing a game. Carl and Moodie, Rat, Ronald, Harold, Edward, Pless, and Ernest. They're playing skillzies. Carl says it makes time go away. He plays it well. Painted the numbers onto the street a few months ago. Painted boxes around the numbers because they were tired of hunting up a piece of chalk every time the game was put together.

Since the numbers were painted, six buildings have vanished on the north side of the block, and a couple of addresses on the south side have been emptied. The people moved into new neighborhoods, helped out by the city, most into equally crowded, landlord-ignored buildings a long way from the block.

The big guys are playing a long game. The neighborhood is being carted away. Carl says it won't be long before this won't be a block any more. Just a street.

Before the block started coming down, there were big guys and little kids—and girls. Most of the little kids and the girls are gone. Most of the big guys moved away, too, but it's easier for them to come by every day or so to see who's around. Most days just about everybody's around who's been around for the last three or four years. The game will go on until the demolition workers and the trucks that carry away the building shards are replaced by builders, steam shovels, and derricks and trucks bringing things in.

The big guys are playing.

Carl says there's plenty of time.

Skillzies, skillies, or skullzies—it sounds different on different blocks. It plays the same; it's one game. Most days on this block it gets going around two in the afternoon. In the heat of the summer it sometimes goes until two or three in the morning. Shots are played out under the mercury lamps long after the pushers at the foot of the block have made their last sale in the early morning and moved on to wherever it is that pushers go to unwind.

Harold says the trick to the game is in the index finger. Good index finger, never far from winning. And there's the piece. Up to the individual player. Poker chips heated to the melting point and welded together one atop the other work well. Ernest says beginners, the little kids, melt candle wax into bottle caps. That's okay for playing on the sidewalks. But in the street the distances are greater, the weight of the chips helps, and on this block on the hill you're aiming up at least half the time. The game goes on. Time is being beaten.

Izzy learned the game on 114th Street. He doesn't play much any more. He says it reminds him too much of golf. You play from number one to thirteen. Then you have to go back from thirteen to one. Not exactly like golf but enough. Rat says no, it's more croquet. Except you go for numbers instead of hoops. And when you hit someone with your piece, instead of sending them, you get yourself a move to your next number and a free shot from that number. Harold says it's pool. You can make a run like in pool. And Moodie's hot. Just skimmed across the street from seven to eight. Dead center, and he's crouching poised for an attack on Ernest's three-tiered chip. Got it! An exaggerated strut to nine, where he crouches and aims. Shooting from nine to ten he nicks Carl, resting a few inches from the number six square, and now he's at tenzies going eleven. Ernest is grimacing. Ernest says, "Moodie, you're getting ahead o'even yourself." He laughs and Moodie snaps one from eighteen inches at Harold, but the piece rises from a wound in the street and skips over the target by less than a chip thickness. Harold stretches his long arms and steps up to begin his move. Carl says watch it. The players and the spectators open a space in the street. A taxi speeding up as it begins the incline whooshes over the game and roars to the intersection.

It's still watchit. Another car is coming up the

hill slowly, a Nova, driven by a tight-mouthed woman who seems to be upholstered in maroon-and-blue plaid. It crawls through the playing area. The woman keeps her eyes focused straight ahead as though she's daydreaming about those tire ads on TV that show erotic-looking women driving alone in thunderstorms and blizzards on lonely tree-bordered stretches of access roads, safe in the knowledge that the car won't break down and let God-knows-what happen to them.

Ernest leans toward the car window inching past him and says, "Lady, if you're gonna stop, we expect you to play." The car jolts forward, and the players without memories of the driver are back into the game immediately. Harold to Carl, Edward, then Ronald complete their turns and tighten up the game.

Ernest says, "Man, if there's one thing I'm not gonna do today it's drink that water." And he begins a five-square run and catches up with Moodie. Since there's not a lot of money around, at least for betting on the game, it often becomes a penalty contest. The winner doesn't have to do anything. But all the losers, one after another, have to drink down a quart of water. Not every time but two or three times a week there'll be a series of water games.

Carl says that if you're not confident of winning you shouldn't play, and if you get beat you
should pay a price. The game goes on. Ernest is
showboating—brandishing a stubby broom,
sweeping out the debris, real and imaginary,
between his piece and his target. Carl is severe
and deep in concentration when it's his turn. The
big guys play it light sometimes, and darkly
others, but they play to win.

ROPES

It's Cuca's turn to jump. Shouts float up the block. A garbage can rattles. A truck wheezes past. Her body moves slowly at first, joining the rhythm of the rope. Her feet pick up the slap-slap-slap of the beat and then, with a darting motion, she moves inside the rope. The beat picks up. The counting starts. One hundred one, one hundred two . . . one hundred ten . . . two hundred one, two hundred two. . . . And as she gains control over the pace, it quickens again until the sounds merge to a slapslapslap-slap as she leaps, turns, leaps, and moves from foot to foot.

High-pitched singsong rhymes begin without a
signal. The words vary slightly from neighborhood to neighborhood, but the giggling is
constant.

Two on time—don't be late,
Your mother got a date
    at a quarter to eight.
If she's late
    she lose her date.

Stam-pede follow me
    to the bottom of the sea.
While you there
    wash your hair
And your dirty underwear.

I see China
I see France
I see a hole—in your pants.
Not too big
Not too small
Just the size of a cannonball.

Double dutch is the most difficult and the fastest.
A double rope swinging as soft eggbeater
blades, moving always toward and always away.

Potatoes-tomatoes, canned peas,
Mother says you have to eat
    a lot of these.

Cabbage, string beans, black-eyed peas,
Mother says you have to eat
    a lot of these.

Hello—hello, hello sir,
Meet me at the grocer.
Yes sir—no sir,
Cause I have a cold sir.
How you get a cold sir?
At the North Pole sir.
Whatcha doin' there sir?
Catchin' Polar Bear sir.
How many did you catch sir?
One sir—two sir—three sir—
  four sir—five sir—six sir—
  seven sir—eight sir—nine sir—
  ten sir—eleven sir—twelve sir—
  thirteen sir—fourteen sir—fifteen sir—
  sixteen sir—seventeen sir—eighteen sir—
  nineteen sir—twenty sir—twenty-one sir—
  twenty-two sir—twenty-three sir—
  twenty-four sir—twenty-five sir—
  twenty-six sir—twenty-seven sir—
  twenty-eight sir—twenty-nine sir—
  thirty sir—thirty-one sir—
  thirty-two sir—thirty-three sir—
  thirty-four sir—thirty-five sir—
  thirty-six sir—thirty-seven sir—
  thirty-eight sir—thirty-nine sir—
  forty sir—forty-one sir—forty-two sir
  forty-three sir—forty-four sir—
  forty-five sir—forty-six sir—
  forty-seven sir—forty-eight sir—
  forty-nine sir—fifty sir—
  fifty-one sir—fifty-two sir—
  fifty-three sir—fifty-four sir—
  fifty-five sir—

TOPS

The season never ends. There are days on a block, even weeks, when tops aren't thrown, but that doesn't mean that their time, like football or even stoopball and stickball, has already come or gone. A simple toy, one of man's oldest, and at Elias's Candy and Sundries they're always in stock. Thirty-five cents—and they come in red, yellow, and blue. The blue ones seem to be most popular. One learns by watching and trying, helped by the hands of fathers or big brothers or guys on the street already tossing.

When they are being thrown—unleashed with intensity and grace—to spin toward a curb or be carefully swept up, still spinning, from the street by an outstretched hand, tops seem a

diversion, worth a glance as you walk by, in the way that a city eye appraises a shop window or a traffic light a few blocks ahead. But to stop and watch is to sometimes see a small aimless moment unfold and briefly become a battle. The battle is a game called crack top. There are block refinements, but basically it is this: it starts with the smallest or weakest or newest or on a given day the least popular top thrower being told to spin his down. The first top spun onto the street becomes, as it defiantly begins its motion, a target surrounded by throwers intent upon smacking it with their tops. With a controlled fury that even the Defense Department would admire, the blitz begins. Top after top is spun down from unraveling strings, aimed at the target top. The customers at Elias's score one point for a hit, two points if they hit and explode a chunk of wood out of the top, and five points if their precision aim and the force of their attacking top shatters the target into pieces.

For the players there are only a few ways out of a game after it's started. It can end for everyone when enough agree that they've had it and it's time to take on something or someone else. Usually there's only one acceptable reason for an individual to leave on his own. That's when such a voice of unquestioned authority as a mother's is heard ordering someone home or to the store or out of the street.

But if a player is just tired of losing and wants to drop out, there is "fifty-two to the toe," a massive penalty that must be considered and quite often paid. All he must do is stand still while tops are flung at his toes fifty-two times. On the street, quitting always has a price.

FLOAT TAG

The small sculpture garden, designed and built as a toddlers' play area next to a playground, was probably an afterthought by the landscape architect or a textbook answer to soften an environment bordered by tall, economically plain apartment houses financed and administered by the government. A nice variation, anyway. A small space in a superblock, less than a hundred yards from main traffic avenues and dotted with ginkgo trees whose leaves summer after summer miraculously offer green highlights while absorbing at least some of the exhaust and smoke fumes that fill the air day after day. The small stone figures surrounded by the low wall have for years submitted to use, and they survive. They're in a city so the moments, good and bad, are part of the deal. It had to be a bad moment when the head of one of the poised horse figures was knocked off. And maybe simple fooling around took care of the edges of the mushroom. But the figures are there. The low brick walls are there. And they've been put into play.

Float tag, less than a national or for that matter even a neighborhood game, started and stayed here. It's played usually as a bridge between talking about what's going on and more famous games. Like every other game of tag, someone is "it." Everyone else is a target. Jumpers are chased, only to be tagged out if they're caught in the air or if they're stationary for more than a three count. It goes on in seeming slow motion, merged into the beat of music rasping sweetly from an ever-present transistor. It softens an afternoon and puts life into brick walls and mottled statues.

RINGOLEVIO

Ringolevio. It is bursts of speed, quickness, exhilaration, durability, cunning, drive. Everything that goes into catching and not being caught. And parked cars, moving cars, street poles, stoops, areaways—all the inanimate things that give proportion to a street—come into play as obstacles to hide behind, dodge, and explode from.

The rules are simple. Two sides of roughly equal size. Each has an area that serves as jail. And each side works to capture and jail all the members of the other team without getting captured themselves. When everyone on one team is in jail, the game is over.

Catching is what it's about. Immobilizing an opponent and then getting him to the jail. A jailed player is expected to try to escape, and if he's not successful at it, he can still be freed—everyone in the jail area can be freed if a teammate makes his way into the area and shouts "Free-All!"

Legend has it that fifteen or twenty years ago there were major ringolevio matches with big-money gambling between neighborhood onlookers. Contests would go on through days and nights covering whole neighborhoods rather than single blocks. Now, with rooftops and abandoned buildings more or less off limits because of junkies, the game has mostly been handed down to younger players. Now instead of formal challenges issued from group to group setting time and place for an official contest, it usually comes out of sidewalk conversation:

"Wanna go shoot baskets?"

"The courts are full. Gotta wait at least an hour."

"Football?"

"Ball's flat."

"Ringolevio?"

"Naah—not enough guys."

"Come on—a lot are over at Edward's house."

"I'll go get Edward."

Because it's a friendly game it's cut in half. There's only one jail, a stoop. One side chases down the other until all are captured. Then the caught become the chasers.

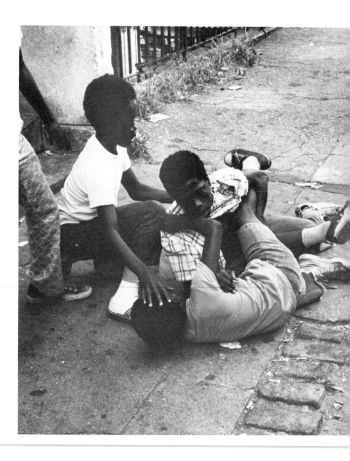

"You gotta determine their weakness. You know, the softest guy. Then it's just a matter of a coupla cracks at 'em and you can collapse 'em." Arnold Walker explains how his Johnny-on-a-pony team, although outweighed by five to ten pounds a man, has just won four out of four. It's not strictly a city game. In grassy suburbs and small towns it's usually called buck buck. To most products of neighborhoods, Johnny on a pony is something that happens in the dead of summer when light and heat stretch well into evening. As with most city events, it contains more form than rules.

At its simplest all that's needed are enough people to make two teams of equal size, and a common drive for victory. For the team that's the pony it's just a matter of planting feet, bending at the waist, hanging on to whoever—the pillow—or whatever is in front, and bracing for the shock of a series of bodies to leap and crash upon their collective backs.

One at a time, the jumpers rush toward the pony, leapfrog the hindmost croucher, and hurtle, legs spread, to straddle and hang on. Another jumper dashes forward, vaults into the air, and adds a jolt with his weight. Another and another until a mass of bodies is locked together. If none of the jumpers slip or fall and the pony team hasn't collapsed, a shout from the jumpers follows: "Johnny on a pony, 1, 2, 3; Johnny on a pony, 1, 2, 3; Johnny on a pony, 1, 2, 3." A scoreless half inning. The roles are traded and so it goes back and forth until either the pony collapses or the jumpers fail to hang on.

The basic tenet: If any player shows a sign of weakness, unload everything on him. "That second one there. His knees are buckling. Gotta all land on him. And this time fast. Start running, man, as soon as the guy in front of you starts his jump." Not surprisingly to anyone who hangs around 103rd Street, he is right. Two rounds later the nearly eight hundred pounds of his team aimed at "the soft one" win out.

HOPSCOTCH

She had been playing hopscotch alone for two hours, pausing every few minutes to pick up a nub of chalk and line out a new grid. She carefully inscribed fresh numbers and then again deliberately and quietly challenged the new spaces, first lofting a rusted number-six nail to her numbered goal and then slowly hopping through the pattern to retrieve the marker and return to the starting line. It was the second Sunday in September, the heart of the afternoon, and she was starting school again the next day. But for now the unusually muted street lined with warehouses and overhung by five- and six-story walk-up apartment houses seemed swallowed in the timelessness that comes with a Sunday afternoon when summer has ended and fall hasn't begun. She moved through the numbers four times, used them up, put down the nail, and again picked up the chalk. She had finished lining out one more framework when her mother leaned out from a fifth-floor window. "C'mon now . . . we gonna have dinner." She answered by looking up, and as her mother stepped away from the window she moved through the chalked boxes and finished her numbering. Then, standing again at start for a moment, she studied the new pattern, picked up the nail, and floated it to a landing in the heart of number ten. She straightened herself, hurried into her building, and clattered up the stairway.

One, two, three, a tiger,

    four, five, six, a tiger,

      seven, eight, nine, a tiger

    ten . . . a ti-ger

All it takes is a small rubber ball and a sidewalk or a wall. If the people at the A. G. Spalding Sporting Goods Company knew how to pronounce their name, they'd probably phoneticize the spelling on the side of the ball—and justly honor the Spaldeen. This small, hollow rubber ball is without question the most important piece of city game equipment. If you follow it bouncing through a city you hear the counting off of rhythms and rhymes and see, to name only a few other games; stoopball, handball, Chinese wallball, boxball, and, when a cut-off broomstick is added, stickball.

One, two, three, a Russian,

    four, five, six, a Russian,

      seven, eight, nine, a Russian,

    ten . . . a Rus-sian.

Miss Lucy had a bra,
  a bra, a bra,
Miss Lucy had a bra,
  and this is what she did . . .

Miss Lucy had a girdle,
  a girdle, a girdle,
Miss Lucy had a girdle,
  and this is what she did . . .

Miss Lucy had a husband,
  a husband, a husband,
Miss Lucy had a husband,
  and this is what she did . . .

Miss Lucy had a baby,
  a baby, a baby,
Miss Lucy had a baby,
  and this is what she did . . .

Miss Lucy's baby died,
  did die, did die,
Miss Lucy's baby died,
  and this is what she did . . .

Miss Lucy's husband he did die,
  did die, did die,
Miss Lucy's husband he did die,
  and this is what she did . . .

Miss Lucy she did die,
  did die, did die,
Miss Lucy she did die,
  and this is what she did . . .

FENCES/BENCHES

When a natural history museum of American industrial cities is finally put together, there are two items which will rank high on the list of important displays: a section of chain-link fencing and a concrete-base, wooden-lattice-backed bench used on sidewalks and in parks. Chain fences can be used a number of ways. Some keep people out; others keep people or things in. You can scale them, walk on top of them, jump over them, and jump into them. There are miles and miles of chain fences in the cities. Somewhere is the man, or at least the heirs to the man, who developed the standard chain-link fence and became both a commercial patron saint of the security industry and the Abner Doubleday of fence players.

Nobody with clout ever said that swings are just for little kids. Norma, Yogi, TaTa, Zsa Zsa, Chuck, Pete, Fred, and Edwin are on the swings at least a couple of times a week. They work them up high—alone, in pairs, or spread five or six over two held-together swings. Pump up to the sky. Chuck says, "It's a feeling of flight. You look down from the top and you're higher than anyone. It's flying.

"When you push yourself up there you can feel a force, but when you get to that point that you're on top—when you can't go up any higher and you're just ready to go down—you feel weightless just for a fragment of a second. You feel like you're floating, standing on air.

"Sometimes I feel like a bird. I go high on the swing and close my eyes and concentrate on just that one thing—that I'm a bird. I concentrate and concentrate—that's me—and when I finish the ride I'm dizzy."

He had forced the swing as high as it could go without doubling over and spilling him onto the ground. And with a languid movement as the swing flew back to the beginning of its arc, he slid from his standing position to a tense sit, and as it ducked and again rose he flew out of the seat to land grasping the metal fence fourteen feet above the ground. He had "jumped the fence."

At first glance, jumping the fence doesn't appear to be the kind of thing that is learned. The first jump has to be successful. Ralph, the jumper, says, though, that three or four years ago, the first time he tried it, he waited too long to leave the swing and flew over the fence, far enough out to miss a metal basketball backboard on the far side on his way down. In his fall he got caught on the basket rim and broke his shoulder. And his little brother—he was seven, and started jumping when he was six —used to jump fences at a different playground. There was no mesh fence there. It had been torn down, but the framework was still standing and the swing riders would jump to the top bar and hang on. His brother left the swing too late, struck the bar with his chest, flipped over, and down. He died two days later. After explaining this, Ralph walked back to the swing for a few more jumps before calling it a day.

PSYCH JOB

Pete Berdeguez invented a game. It's called psych job because the first time he demonstrated it one of the original players blurted out, "Man, this is some psych job." He invented it early one evening after shooting baskets alone at the bent metal backboard in the foot of a pocket park. Two years earlier, forty thousand dollars in landscaping design and construction had been spent on a narrow, junk-cluttered empty lot that separated two old tenements. That was the summer that ecology and working-with-kids was understood to be an excellent promotional vehicle for big companies. And the advertising promotion department from a magazine and some advertising agency people became active, rounded up donations, and found a dead lot. By the time the publicity photographers and TV news teams could assemble, the transformation was complete: at the street front a small basketball area, benches, overhead monkey bars, a slide, concrete checkerboards, and more benches. When Pete invented his game he was standing next to the brick wall directly under the exercise bars. He flipped his basketball at an angle through the space between the last bar and the wall and watched it carom off the wall and bounce back onto the bars, thumping back and forth unpredictably from bar to bar before it fell down cleanly between bars. The game was invented. The next day Pete was bouncing a Spaldeen instead of a basketball and again flipped it up. Pete's rules, and they are the only ones, are that any number of people can crowd under the bars and, looking up—you have to look up—jostle for position to grab the ball when it stops bouncing and drops through. There's no scoring, but if you catch it then it's your turn to fling it off the bricks to the top of the bars. And you keep your serve until someone makes a catch.

The game has changed slightly since the beginning. Change was forced because the building that served as the back wall for the psych job area—and as a side wall for the pocket park—fell down. Most of it fell on top of the park. The building had been empty for months after a three-alarm fire had gutted it. Maybe "fell" isn't the right word. It's rumored around the block that it was knocked down. During the weeks before the collapse, a human-body-shaped hole above the third floor of the building's park side grew in silhouette day after day. Then, the afternoon that a thumping was heard coming from the building, a few bricks spilled down, enlarging the shape's left leg. With a rumble the five-story, ninety-year-old building groaned and slowly fell down. Two people were seen suspended from the still-hanging wooden beams as the dust settled throughout the block. No one was hurt and on the block everyone knows not to pay attention to rumors. The important thing is that once the rubble was partially cleared away the park area, although dustier, was twice as big. And the psych job players quickly learned how to play a ball falling off behind the bars.

STOOPBALL

Stoopball borrowed the framework and language of baseball. And the streets began echoing the thwacks of a ball caroming off cement steps and building faces in the days when baseball was truly the national game and stars' names like Honus Wagner, Napy Lajoie, and the Babe rolled off the tongues of kids throughout the nation's cities. Over the years stoopball and stickball have hung on. Stoopball is usually picked up first. It's easier for a little kid to throw a ball than to smack one with a broomstick bat. Symmetry, tension, and flow are as present in this condensed form on the streets and sidewalks as in any temperature-controlled, all-weather, domed big-league amphitheater. The result compresses a game of combed dirt and manicured green open spaces into a narrow, obstacle-filled street. Instead of a pitcher, a hitter, and a bat, the stoopball hitter flings the ball into play. He throws hard into the crease where the sidewalk and the cement step meet or, more often these days, where a concrete wall joins the sidewalk. Then, depending on what particular block the game's played on, it goes this way: If the ball rebounds fair and is caught on the fly or on the rebound from the backdrop building, it's an out. If it's foul, it's out automatically.

If there are enough players on a side, usually three or four, the hits can be run out over the chalked outlines of bases marked temporarily on the streets and sidewalks. But often, instead of running out hits, each bounce of the ball before it's caught represents a base. Two bounces are a double, three a triple. And again, depending on the specific block, when a Spaldeen rises from the hard edge of the sidewalk and lofts up high, usually above the second or third floor of the buildings in what would be center field, a

home run has just been scored.

The changes in city architecture, the project houses with interior courts and sidewalks, have dictated change in famous games like stoopball and stickball. The games have been kept alive because from the beginning they have been ingenious weddings of big sports and limited spaces. The spaces change, but imagination and energy are all it takes to keep up with a city and fit a game into a new setting.

Stickball's a little closer to the big game than stoopball. Instead of playing the width of a street, it stretches down the block as far as a hollow Spaldeen can be powered with a cut-off broom handle. It's often an impressive distance. There are neighborhood variations upon variations. If there's a basic version it's the street game—the hitter flipping the ball into the air, fixedly eyeing its bounce in front of him, and then, as it rises to its apex, stepping into the ball to slash at it with the bat. When the ball is smashed into the playing area, the standard baseball rules take over—again with variations. A ball landing and staying on a rooftop—fair or foul—is an automatic out. But a fair ball skimming off fire escapes, window frames, and dribbling down building faces is in play. There's a version of the game called slow pitch which, with a pitcher, becomes baseball except for the size of the ball and the narrow bat. And there's "off the wall," a tailoring of the classic to interior courtyards, a reversed mirror-image form. The pitcher stands behind the batter, outfielders ranging behind them and all facing the same wall, as the batter waits for his crack until a pitch has been flung at the wall and rebounds to him. His hit is in play the moment that, on the fly, it again strikes the wall. Then stoopball bounce rules take over. One bounce before being caught is a single, and a home run is four bounces or a smash hopelessly beyond reach of the defenders.

PROPERTY OF
TAKOMA PARK, MD. LIBRARY
83307

HANDBALL

Handball, the indoor four-wall game, has been ritualized by athletic clubs and associations as a white-collar, keeping-in-shape game with championships of varying magnitude played out in the recesses of dark-paneled formal clubs. It seems to play better, however, be more alive, and offer more as a game without pretense or artifice, surrounded by the city's sounds and smells. It only requires a bare wall, a Spaldeen, and players—anyone who can move and wants to whack a ball with an open palm.

CHINESE WALLBALL

Good handball is a combination of power and finesse. Chinese wallball is a statement of pure finesse. At least three, four, or five players poise facing a stretch of wall and cut delicate quick shots back and forth. One bounce to the wall. Then it angles off the wall to other players stretching for short, low, crisp shots, slapping and slapping off the wall from player to player until one misses. That's a point lost, and it moves the player who came up short to the end of the line farther from the server who, on the far left of the line facing the wall, puts the ball in play again. He's where everyone else wants to be, because he's safe from losing points as long as he maintains his serve. Until he muffs a shot and loses his serve, not a point, and takes up the last place on the line, he's invulnerable. When a given game is five points and out, meaning the field is slowly cut down each time a player has lost five points until only one player remains, what it's all about is getting and keeping the serve—being invulnerable.

Boxball is Ping-Pong without a net or a table or paddles, and a Spaldeen instead of a brittle Ping-Pong ball. All it takes are two sidewalk squares or a piece of chalk or some tape, good quick hands, and concentration. Throughout any real city there are plenty of sidewalks, and Spaldeens, and countless good quick hands.

BASKETBALL

Thoughts on learning by a fifteen-year-old journeyman ballplayer:

"We're out there—rain, snow, anything— playing basketball. That's the only way you're gonna learn. If you wait till the summer, I mean, you'll be the lousiest people around. From stoopball I came into basketball, because I was really interested in the sport when I saw it. I was about ten, I guess. I watched guys playing. I said I gotta learn, too, to be with my friends. You know, on our block if you don't know how to play basketball you can't hang out. 'Cause that's all they do. Take a ball and shoot it. So that's why I said to myself I gotta learn.

"At first Chicky and me learned on our own. I never wanted the guys to teach me how to play. I wanted to surprise them. In the beginning mainly when the guys played I used to sit down, watch them play, and see how they would do it, and when I practiced I'd try to do what they did as best I could.

"We practiced in the winter. We had this little shovel and we used to shovel for hours 'cause it was ice-hard. We'd clean out a space and then bounce the ball and shoot it all day. At first in the summertime, if we did have a ball, we wouldn't play on the block. We'd walk around somewhere and find an empty court and shoot there where we could be alone. That was a long time ago.

"Now I look at the pros. If they can do it anybody else can. Not dunk it, but you know if they could do any ordinary thing we can do it—dribble the ball—shoot the ball—smash people. The only thing they can do is, they're taller and they know how to do it better than we do. I've never, never in my life gotten tired of basketball. I never will. It's THE game."

FOOTBALL

The streets aren't big enough for it. And unlike baseball, which could be cut down to stoopball and stickball, football can't exist without space. Sure, there are some small-scale pick-up touch games compressed into the width of a sidewalk or erratically played on the street. It's for the little kids. They have to learn to throw and catch and stop a ballcarrier somewhere because until they do they won't be asked into the real games, the games that begin when, with the middle of September, the season arrives. It's then that block and neighborhood teams are put together and "leagues" are loosely formed. Tactics are discussed and determined with the language of the pro television commentators on stoops and in neighborhood clubrooms. Games are scheduled. Then much of the action moves onto the Tarmac- and asphalt-surfaced playgrounds where crushed glass becomes as big a problem as a pair of blitzing linebackers.

It's not tackle.

It makes more sense to think of it as grab football rather than touch. The point on defense is to make it impossible for a ballcarrier to move. On offense, it's to make big plays and score and score and score and score.

STREET HOCKEY

It took three seasons to get the hockey equipment together. Sticks and a regulation puck that first winter, triggered by an unexpected blizzard that closed schools for three days and not incidentally kept traffic off the street. Most of the players were in junior high school then.

The second season, goalie pads were added and the puck was tossed aside for a roll of electrician's tape. It was easier on the shins. The third fall, it was masks for the goalies and a collapsible aluminum-framed goal net. There would have been a second net by the end of the year but Ronald, the real force behind the block's hockey games and the original buyer of most of the equipment, moved out of the neighborhood and no one stepped into his place as promoter. But the games continue sporadically during the cold weather. In the city-fringe neighborhoods that bridge the gap between blocks and suburbs, it is more organized. There, the game is usually played on roller skates, often in official leagues with referees, timekeepers, judges, and teams with facsimile pro uniforms and protective pads for everyone.

Ronald got everybody on roller skates for a game early in the second season, but it turned into a disaster. Parked cars almost never come out second best when body-checked, so the skates followed the hard rubber puck to the sidelines. But good smart stickwork, rough defense, darting moves into an imagined crease for strong slap shots on goal, and brash, gutsy challenges by the goalies are there, every time a game is put together.

PIGEONS

Walking.

Climbing.

Up six flights of narrow, dark stairs to the roof of a tenement. The metal-sheathed door to the roof has to be forced open; its armament has added a half inch to its width that the doorframe wasn't built to handle. Outside on the roof, from atop the spongy tarpaper-covered flat surface, the city isn't bad. Proportions are better. The erupting project apartment buildings taking the place of old neighborhoods reach up but can't block out the sky.

Not too many years ago rooftops belonged to the people who lived beneath them. In those days the odds were against finding a neighborhood block where you could scramble the length of the connected roofs without coming upon at least one pigeon coop. It's different now. In most neighborhoods the roofs have been abandoned and given over unwillingly to junkies for their occasional use. And in the new project apartment buildings there are no rooftops. There are just the tops of tall buildings with cement sheds housing water towers and elevator cables— "Off limits to all unauthorized personnel." With the loss of so many roofs, coop pigeons, the well-tended rooftop flocks, have become an exception rather than a constant. But scattered throughout the city men and boys still work their flocks for two or three hours a day, every day. Opening the gate to let the softly cooing birds up into the sky. Whistling them up, higher and higher, into and over the skyline.

Wiso says it takes him over a year to really establish a new bird with his flock. He started flying pigeons when he was twelve, and now he has sons who share his love for the birds—and the rooftops. Every afternoon they're on the roof feeding and flying the birds, watching them as they hook in widening circles overhead, beating a heady rhythm through the seasons.

There are four other flocks within eight blocks of Wiso's coop, and moments come when he lets his birds rise to the challenge of a neighboring flock. It's a ritualized duel as the keepers, unseen by each other, whistle their birds into widening arcs until they near each other.

Then, with good luck and bad, a few birds

will slip off from one group and join the other. Flying with them at the shrill whistle from the trainer to return to the coop as rookie members of a flock. They're kept if they're up to a flock's standards. If not they are often turned in at the local petshop as a down payment on a solid bird, or simply given over for the going wholesale price of a dollar and a half. If a run-of-the-mill city pigeon, a clinker, joins with a flock it's shoved out of the roost to return to the statues and office buildings. Wiso's birds—most of the roof birds—are in the middle of dove and pigeon lineage between the statue-sitting clinkers and the aristocratic homing pigeons. But on the rooftop, with street sounds slightly muffled and skies open, exactly where the birds stand in a biological hierarchy is a small matter. What is important is that they are alive, flying with strength and beauty, floating in circle after circle like kites without strings before returning to their home coop for the night.

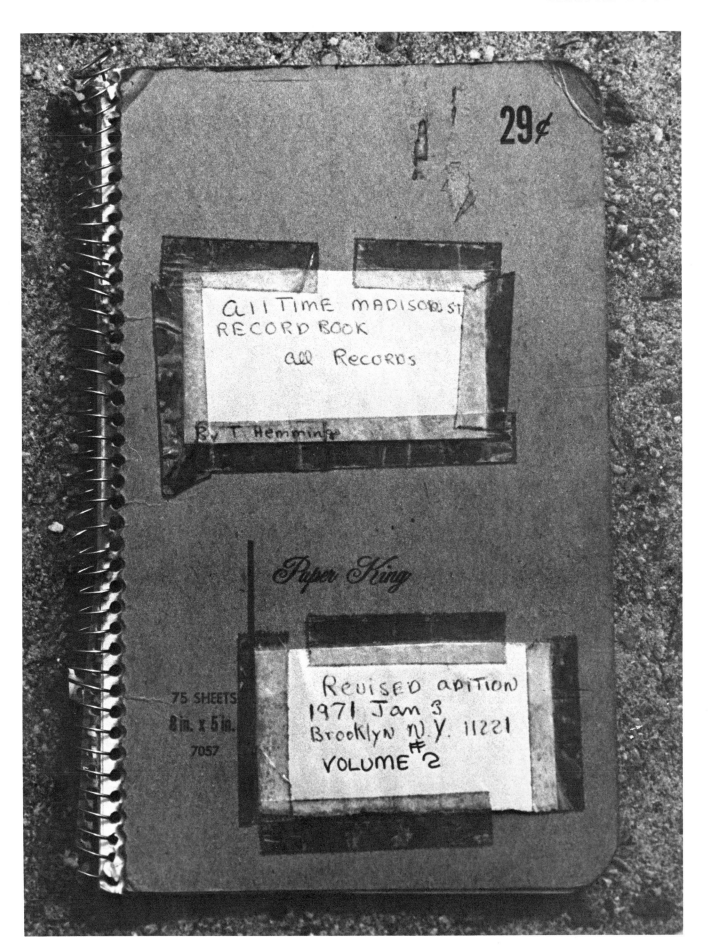

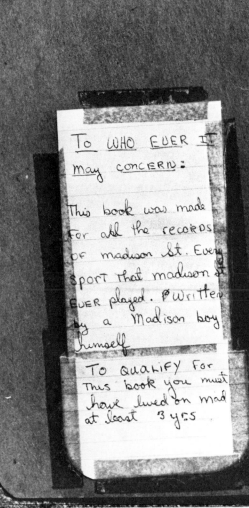

TO WHO EVER IT
May CONCERN:

This book was made
for all the records
of madison St. Every
sport that madison St
EVER played. Written
by a Madison boy
himself

TO QUALIFY FOR
This book you must
have lived on mad
at least 3 yrs

INDEX

ALL Time MAD MGR
DAVE HEMMINGS 24-3
7-1 1968
7-1 1969
10-1 1970

ALLTime BASEBALL (HARD)
1B - Denis BARbera   C - Ricky Walker
2B - Charles PeARSON   RH - Oscar Colon
SS - Jim Bou   LH - J. ATKinson
3B - Tom Mimes   CF - Tom Hemming
LF - Jose Colon   RF - Jeff Cusion

AllTime BASKETBall Team
F - Tom (AMAZIN) Hemmings G. J. Bou
F - T. Mimes C - R. WAIKeR G - C. PEARSON

ALLTime HOCKeY TEAM
F - Tom Hemmin F R. Goodwyn D T. M.mes
F Jose Colon D - O. Colon   G R. Mewborn

UMPIRES
Tom Hemmings   J. BOU
O. Colon

AllTime SOFTBALL TeAM
C Ron GOODWYN   3B T. Mimes
1B R. WAIReR
P T. Aemmings LF J. ATK J. Colon
2B Charles Pearson CF O. Colon
SS J. Bou   RF PATe, Cushion